Name

....

Year

....

Banksias
Uniquely Australian plants bearing large yellow
to red upright bottle-brush flowers.

Bilbies
Attractive, long-eared, desert marsupials which
dig burrows beside spinifex clumps. A popular
Easter symbol in Australia. Endangered.

SPECIAL NOTE
The seasonal patterns and sequences of natural
events described in this book will not always occur
exactly as forecast. There will naturally be variation
from year to year and place to place. Your own
observations are valuable to the Gould League's
Timelines Project as we explore Australia's seasons
and record environmental data. Eventually this
information will be used to predict and name
seasonal patterns, so that land management
practices and environmental monitoring can be
better attuned to our unique continent.

Banksias
~ and ~
Bilbies
Seasons of Australia

A weekly guide to natural events in Australia,
with space for your own records.

Gouldian finches

Gould League

Written and researched by Alan Reid
Illustrated by Alexis Beckett
Editor Jim Grant

BANKSIAS AND BILBIES

Author: Alan Reid
Illustrator: Alexis Beckett
Editor: Jim Grant
Typesetting: Alan Mayberry & Jo-Anne Ridgway — Polar Design
Charts and diagrams: Steve Blackie — Polar Design

Published by the Gould League of Victoria Inc.
Genoa Street, Moorabbin, Victoria, Australia 3189
Phone: (03) 9532 0909
Fax: (03) 9532 2860
Modem: (03) 9553 5049

GOULD LEAGUE
OF VICTORIA INC
Educating for the Environment

Gould League publications are prepared with the assistance of staff and other resources provided by the Directorate of School Education, Victoria.

Cataloguing in publication data

Reid, A. J. (Alan J.).
    Banksias & Bilbies: Seasons of Australia: a weekly guide to natural events in Australia, with space for your own records.

    Includes index.
    ISBN 1 875687 26 2.

    1. Natural history – Australia.   2. Seasons – Australia.
    1. Beckett, Alexis.   II. Gould League of Victoria.

508.94

Further copies are available from the Gould League Bookshop, Genoa Street, Moorabbin 3189.

Printed on environmentally friendly paper.

ACKNOWLEDGMENTS

The author gratefully acknowledges the assistance of the following people over the past nine years:

Queen Elizabeth II Silver Jubilee Trust; Nigel Tucker, QNPS; John Squires, Kuranda; Kaye Alderhoven, Jabiru; Steven Davis, Milingimbi; Stuart Traynor, CCNT; Jean Sims, Alice Springs; Noreen and George Brown, Darwin; Eric McCrum, Perth; Clem Gullick, Noonamah; Janice Jones, Alice Springs; children of Braitling Primary School; Renee Steel, Cairns; Alan Webb, Townsville; Dot Kingston, Derby; Glenis Taylor, Daly River; children of Milner School; children of Humpty Doo School; Dawn Margay, Meg Evans and John Smith, Cairns; children of Dampier Downs Station; Don Haupt and children of Woree School, Cairns; John G. Reid, Jabiru; children of Beverly Hills Station, Derby; John and Sue Erbacher, Hervey Bay; Bob Winters, Alan Mayberry, Pat Armstrong and Gayle Seddon of the Gould League; Marc Gottsch, Ken Simpson, Cecily Falkingham, Pat and Ed Gray, John Reid, Elizabeth Sevior, Glen Jameson, Pat Fricker, Trevor Pescott, and Malcolm Calder of the Timelines Committee, Dominic Farnworth, Currumbin Sanctuary; CALM, WA; Jean Edgecombe, Sydney.

I also acknowledge the Aboriginal people whose understanding of seasonal patterns over thousands of years has stimulated the production of this book. I refer particularly to the Wunumbal people of the Kimberley, the Yolngu people of northeast Arnhem Land and the Bunitj people of Kakadu.

Natural Timelines

Knowledge of regular yearly patterns of natural events, such as the times at which plants flower, birds nest, butterflies emerge, and migrants arrive and depart, has been vital to humans for hundreds of thousands of years. The relative times at which these seasonal events take place depend upon factors such as how close a region is to the sea, the strength and direction of prevailing winds, the frequency of fires, the slope of the land, the amount of rainfall, the surface water, and, of course, the species of plants and animals that live there. Naturally people in different parts of the world recognise very different seasons.

In Australia, Aboriginal survival depended upon a knowledge of the sequence of significant natural events, especially those relating to life cycles of useful plants and animals. This Aurukun food timeline from Northern Queensland shows the importance of the sequence of natural events for people living in harmony with the land.

JANUARY	Mud crabs on high tide Green turtles in bay Freshwater sharks coming down rivers
FEBRUARY	Wild grapes are ripe Fruit bats in mangroves
MARCH	Prawns in river Nuts on swamp grass roots
APRIL	Eggs in scrub fowl mounds Fish are fat, geese are thin
MAY	Wild honey sugar bags as bloodwood blooms
JUNE	Yams are ready for cooking Dig for arrowroot
JULY	Turtles lay eggs Lily roots are cooked
AUGUST	Stingrays are fat Mud shells at low tide
SEPTEMBER	Big catfish up river Emu eggs for old people Tree monitors nesting
OCTOBER	Freshwater turtles in mud Fruit bats in mangroves
NOVEMBER	Oysters are ready Black ducks in swamps
DECEMBER	Geese and ducks on plains

Red flowering kurrajong

Aboriginal Seasonal Calendars

Aboriginal calendars relate to local sequences of natural events. Many tribal calendars in Northern Australia still remain in effective use but those in the south have largely been destroyed, along with many of the people and cultures who developed them over thousands of years.

These diagrams show some seasonal frameworks from different parts of Australia. Note the small differences between the calendars of Aurukun and Weipa, only eighty kilometres apart, and the large differences between these and the inland Kakadu, on the same latitude, but over 900 km to the west. Comparisons with the Kimberley seasons show even greater differences.

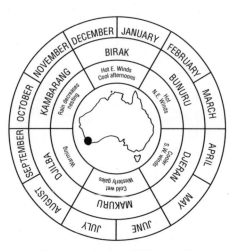

Nyungar calendar of SW Australia showing six seasons

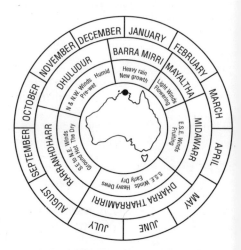

*Yolngu calendar of NE Arnhemland showing six seasons
(Two short sub-seasons are not depicted.)*

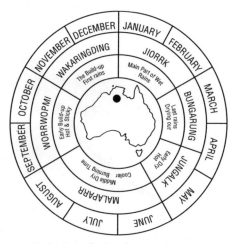

Katherine calendar showing six seasons

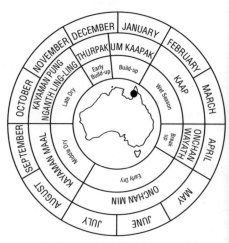

Aurukun calendar on Cape York showing seven seasons

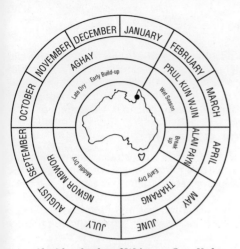

Alngith calendar of Weipa on Cape York showing five seasons

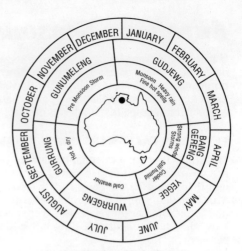

Bunitj calendar of Kakadu region showing six seasons

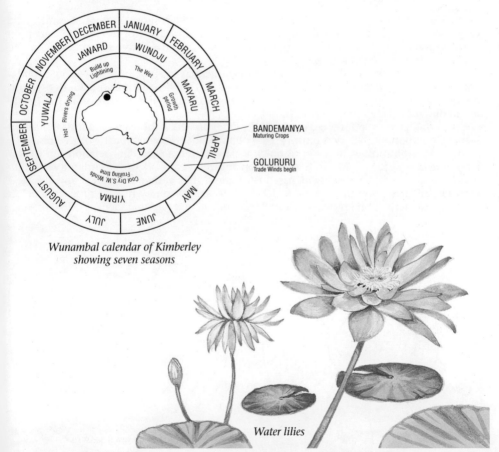

Wunambal calendar of Kimberley showing seven seasons

Water lilies

European Seasons

Urban people from European cultures usually relate seasons to a framework of particular dates and weather patterns, but our seasons originally related to natural events rather than numbered days of the year. Bursts of flowering and nesting, falling of leaves, falls of snow, times for ploughing or harvesting, and changes in day length were recognised, named, and celebrated in Europe for thousands of years before our present calendar was designed.

EUROPEAN CALENDARS DON'T WORK FOR AUSTRALIA

The British brought a calendar of four seasons of equal length to Australia. (In Australia the first day of each season was moved from the solstice or equinox back to the first day of the month for bureaucratic reasons). This calendar is appropriate to their small temperate islands with their fairly regular seasonal patterns, but it certainly does not match the climate of northern Australia, and relates only very roughly to the natural seasons of southern Australia. Most Aboriginal calendars had from five to seven seasons by which activities were carefully planned.

In northern Australia a basic pattern of six seasons is now well recognised and widely used. It is based around wet and dry seasons rather than summer and winter, but in the south the old European calendars are still imposed onto our wide-ranging and very un-European climates.

In recent years several people have attempted to design more appropriate and useful calendars for their regions. For example naturalist Stuart Traynor, of the Conservation Commission of the Northern Territory, has compiled a calendar of five seasons from natural event data in the Darwin region.

In the south, Alan Reid has suggested a new calendar of six seasons based on a similar analysis of extensive local records. Fr. David Ranson has published a proposal for five seasons for an area further up the Yarra Valley, in an attempt to relate European Christian spirituality to our different climate.

The number and names of seasons, and the dates on which they start and finish, may not seem very important, but our continued use of a calendar designed for the other side of the world is an indication of how out of touch we are with our land. Our relationship with it reflects an imposition of old habits, rather than an attempt to work with its unique variability and extremes. Land management based on natural data rather than rigid and hopeless expectations may result in land use which is more sensible and sensitive, producing better outcomes for agriculture, recreation, fisheries, tourism, and national identity.

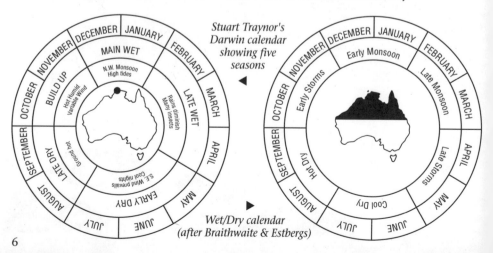

Stuart Traynor's Darwin calendar showing five seasons

Wet/Dry calendar (after Braithwaite & Estbergs)

An Example of a New Calendar

Residents of Melbourne have known for a long time that the European calendar does not match their seasons, even though they experience probably the most European climate of any Australian capital city. Because knowledge of Aboriginal seasons appears to have been lost for this area, the Field Naturalists Club of Victoria, the Gould League, and Melbourne Parks and Waterways have attempted to recreate natural seasons for at least some parts of the Metropolitan area.

Using a vast amount of natural events data, collected by many people over many years in diaries and logbooks, the naturalists determined when natural events clumped into bursts of flowering, seeding or changed animal behaviour, and were able to define six natural seasons for the Melbourne region. Old and new calendars are compared in these diagrams.

How the seasons have changed

1. Autumn does not begin until the weather really starts to cool, after the equinox in late March, when many birds form flocks and start their migration north.
2. Winter begins on the first day of June as it does at present, and is characterised by short days, (the shortest day is in the middle of this season), cold, rough seas, and visits by Antarctic birds.
3. Winter is cut short by a new season, Pre-spring, introduced by the flowering of wattles and early nesting of birds in late July.
4. Spring now begins a week earlier, during the third week in August. This season is characterised by strong winds, rain, rapid growth, and many nesting birds.
5. Early Summer, (second week of November to the third week in January), characterised by birds feeding young and plants seeding, is similar to that experienced by the British.
6. Late Summer is separated by natural events in the new calendar. Hot, sunny weather, interrupted by a series of electrical storms, brings on the hatching of swarms of insects. Melbourne school children regularly return to classes for the most stifling part of the year which lasts into March. This is reflected in the new season which does not give way to Autumn until the third week of that month.

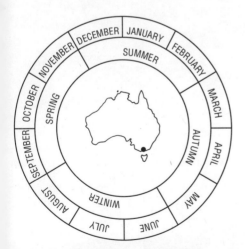

Traditional European calendar

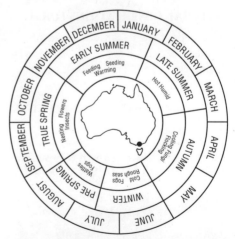

Alan Reid's calendar for the Middle Yarra Region of Melbourne showing six seasons

7

Australia's True Seasons — The Timelines Project

This major program is designed so that all Australians can contribute to a database which can be used to identify the true seasons of Australia, and monitor changes in numbers and distributions of animals and plants. This data will reveal environmental change and possibly climatic trends, and will be used to create better management strategies for our land and wildlife.

Already a great deal of information has been collected from the diaries and logbooks of Australian nature enthusiasts, and we hope to add more of these valuable records to our computer database.

Your own observations are very important

Your records of times of flowering, nesting, etc. in your area, and accounts of unusual natural events will make a very useful contribution to this project. If you keep records in this book, summarise them on the Gould League's Significant Events Report Form at the end of the year, and send it to the Gould League.

What is worth recording?

Almost anything which you find interesting is worth recording, as long as you record why it is of interest.
Especially significant are:

- When something happens for the first or last time for the year.
- When numbers of something reach a peak or trough.
- Results of a natural or human-caused catastrophe, (e.g. fire, storm, flood, bulldozing).
- Distribution change in plant or animal population, (e.g. migration, new record).
- Major behavioural changes in animal behaviour, (e.g. courting, nesting).
- Links between events (e.g. humid weather, thunderstorms, termite hatches, swifts overhead).

A sample natural observations form is shown below. These forms are available from the Gould League.

NATURAL OBSERVATIONS FORM

Recorder's Name ....
Address.. Postcode ....
Phone No. ....

SIGNIFICANT EVENT REPORT FORM — SAMPLE ENTRIES

[essential details for computer entry]

Date Time	Nearest Town & Postcode or Lat/Long or AMG ref.	Vegetation Code	Weather Code	Action Code
311094	Glenburn 3717 or 37.25', 145.27' or 7923 63–56	BO2	A	9
200363	Victoria Valley 3294 37.21', 142.21'	BO4	A	3

Recording Data for the Timelines Project

Use of the codes listed on the following pages will make data entry for the Timelines Project far easier, but written records or letters are very acceptable. When describing the location in country areas record the distance and direction from the nearest town, e.g. 27 km NW of Oodnadatta.

VEGETATION/HABITAT CODES

Category A: densely vegetated (70-100% Cover)	A01:	tall closed forest	trees > 30m
	A02:	closed forest	trees 10-30m
	A03:	low closed forest	trees 5-10m
	A04:	closed scrub	shrubs 2-8m
	A05:	closed heathland	shrubs 0-2m
	A06:	closed fernland	ferns, sedges

Category B: moderately vegetated (30-70% cover)	B01:	tall open forest	trees > 30m
	B02:	open forest	trees 10-30m
	B03:	low open forest	trees 5-10m
	B04:	open scrub	shrubs 2-8m
	B05:	open heath	shrubs 0-2m
	B06:	tussock grassland	grasses < 2m

Category C: sparsely vegetated (10-30% cover)	C01:	tall woodland	trees > 30m
	C02:	woodland	trees 10-30m
	C03:	low woodland	trees 5-10m
	C04:	tall shrubland	shrubs 2-8m
	C05:	low shrubland	shrubs 0-2m
	C06:	hummock grassland (e.g. spinifex)	grasses <2m
	C07:	open tussock	grassland grass tussocks

[this information should be retained for reference]

Species involved	Count Code	Event Description in Detail
Turquoise Parrot	*1AF*	*Female Turquoise Parrot feeding on lawn of Graceburn property – seen by Alan Reid.*
Common Death Adder	*1A*	*Death Adder lay coiled at base of small shrub in open heath scrub – seen by Alan Reid & Ivan McInnes.*

CODES (continued)

Category D:	D01:	tall open woodland	trees > 30m
very sparsely vegetated	D02:	open woodland	trees 10-30m
(less than 10% cover)	D03:	low open woodland	trees 5-10m
	D04:	tall open shrubland	shrubs 2-8m
	D05:	low open shrubland	shrubs 0-2m
	D06:	open hummock grassland	grasses

Category E:	E01:	farmland	cultivated farmland
cultivated or	E02:	urban parkland	community parks etc.
modified vegetation	E03:	house garden	

| Category F: | F01: | swamps, ponds, lakes, marshes, reedbanks |
| wetlands | | |

Category G:	G01:	over sea
	G02:	beach
	G03:	estuary

WEATHER CODES

A: little or no cloud cover, temperate to warm, no or light breeze
B: Little or no cloud cover, cool or very cold, light to strong breeze
C: Much cloud cover, cool, strong gusty winds
D: Overcast, light drizzle to persistent rain, light breeze to gusty winds
E: Little or no cloud cover, hot and dry, light breeze to gusty winds
F: Cloud cover and winds variable, hot and humid conditions
G: Other weather conditions (Please describe)

ACTION CODES

1. Moving quickly
2. Moving slowly
3. Not moving
4. Flying/gliding
5. Hopping/jumping
6. Swimming/floating
7. Building
8. Digging
9. Feeding
10. Preening/grooming
11. Displaying
12. Attacking
13. Defending
14. Defecating
15. Courting/mating
16. Incubating
17. Bearing/hatching
18. Carrying
19. Tracking/chasing
20. Emerging/budding/shooting
21. Flowering
22. Seeding/fruiting
23. Dispersing
24. Dying/dead
25. Hollowed
26. Damaged/diseased

COUNT CODES

Record the actual number seen and follow it with the appropriate age and gender symbols.

(e.g.) 2AM = Two adult males

A - Adult (sex unknown)
J - Juvenile
M - Male
F - Female

10

Australian Habitat Types

Australia is a vast land of incredible diversity. Spectacular wild landscapes include our beautiful tropical rainforests, snow covered mountains and superb beaches. The beauty of our dry country with its mallee, mulga, and bluebush is more subtle. Unfortunately travellers through our continent will experience many landscapes which have been devastated by introduced rabbits and overgrazing by stock, but even in these areas some wildlife survives.

These pages provide a basic vegetation map and very simple guide to most of the habitats referred to in this book.

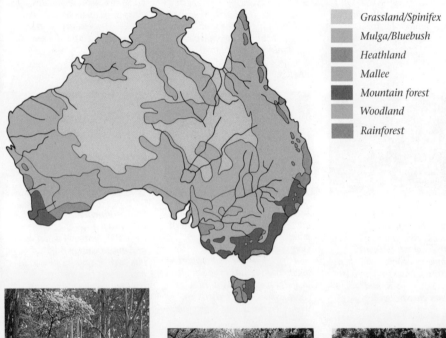

Grassland/Spinifex

Mulga/Bluebush

Heathland

Mallee

Mountain forest

Woodland

Rainforest

Mountain forest: *This tall southern forest type is dominated by tall eucalypts including mountain ash, (A mountain ash in Gippsland was the tallest tree in the world until it was cut down last century) Alpine ash, and stringybarks. The understorey includes Pomaderris, tree ferns, mint bushes, hill banksias, ferns and brackens.*

Temperate rainforest: *Antarctic beech, sassafras, lilly-pilly, clematis and tree ferns dominate these green mossy forests which have survived for millions of years in cool wet areas.*

Photos: Marc Gottsch

Tropical rainforest: *Patches of this spectacular northern habitat have survived clearing, and many are now protected. Figs, Australian cedar, Araucaria pines and a diverse array of other tall trees are entwined with vines and decorated with epiphytic orchids and ferns.*

11

Mallee: Multi-stemmed eucalypts often with scattered areas of callitris (native cypress), sheoaks (casuarina), broombush, spinifex, wilga and bullock-bush.

Monsoon forest: Sometimes called "dry rainforest", this vegetation type can be found in areas which flood and dry out at different times of the year. They are characterised by paperbarks, pandanus palms, epiphytic orchids, vines, native figs and myrtles.

Northern woodland: Open wooded country with ghost gums, pandanus, termite mounds, spear grasses, bush apples, and native plums. This country is often "burned off" in the dry season.

Southern woodland: Drier woodland characterised by stringybark, box, gum, and ironbark eucalypts with an understorey of acacia, wild cherry (Exocarpus), bracken fern, bush peas, tussock grasses, and sometimes grasstrees.

Inland gorges: Livistona palms are the most noticeable feature of many northern inland gorges. Gorges are typically moist areas in a dry landscape and support a distinctive vegetation which often includes river red gums, acacias, caper bushes, parakeelya, corkwoods, cadjeput, and indigofora.

Mulga/bluebush: This habitat covers vast areas of central Australia. Scattered desert oaks and mulga emerge from saltbush, bluebush or spinifex plains. In many areas overgrazing has rendered this habitat almost lifeless by removing the understorey and preventing regeneration of mulga.

Heathland: This stunted low vegetation type occurs in coastal and alpine areas. Near the coast it often consists a of a mixture of button-grass, beard heaths, banksias, sheoaks, small eucalypts, hakeas and grasstrees. In the alps daisies, grasses, sedges, mosses and heaths are important species.

Dry grassland/spinifex: Grassland interspersed with very few trees covers much of the inland. Mitchell grass or spear grass dominate in areas which are seasonally wet, while spinifex dominates drier areas and dunes.

Mangroves: Muddy areas of our coast are often covered with mangroves in the form of trees or bushes. These highly productive areas are home to many communities of animals including invertebrates, fish, birds and reptiles. Although they are difficult to access they are fascinating areas.

Local Environmental Monitoring

Analysis of your diary records will not only show repeated seasonal patterns, but will reveal long-term developmental changes. These changes often happen so slowly that they are only noticed by people who have not visited an area for many years. Recording and noticing this type of change is important so that environmental degradation is not allowed to proceed unnoticed, and so that environmental work is rewarded and able to be used as an inspiration for others. There are many methods of recording long-term change in your area.

An excellent method of recording long-term changes in your area is the regular use of permanent photo points. These can show you how fast things change, the life span of individual plants, and whether vegetation is changing in its size and complexity. The photos below show changes in the ponds at Alan Reid's Glenburn property over a period of eight years.

PHOTOS OF GLENBURN LAKE

1986

1994

SAMPLING HABITATS USING TRANSECTS

One way to sample animal and plant populations is to walk along transect lines or transect belts across different habitats. If you are making a census you can count all the individuals that the line intercepts or the belt encloses.

Transect lines sampling three different habitats.

Belt transect of known length and width.

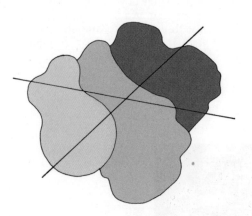
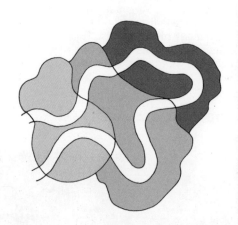

Example of a belt transect census with sample results.
Here are four census counts taken one month apart at 10.30 am at Glenburn in Victorian tall woodland. The walk is about 1km and takes about 30 minutes.

Species	20 Jan.	21 Feb.	18 March	22 April
Cabbage white	1		3	1
Imperial White		1	1	
Shouldered brown		21	43	2
Common grass blue	13	12	5	2
Pea blue	1			
Common brown	4	3	1	1
Sword grass brown	2	2	1	
Ringed Xenica	6	2	1	
Silver Xenica			3	
Klug's Xenicia	91	131	27	

CHECKLISTING

Another simple method of maintaining a change watch on your area is to make general or specific checklists of visible aspects of wildlife at regular intervals.

A wattle flowering checklist at Narre Warren North, Victoria.

Species	J	F	M	A	M	J	J	A	S	O	N	D
A. pycnantha				X	X	X	X	X				
A. boormanii						X	X	X	X			
A. baileyana							X	X				
A. retinoides	X	X	X	X	X	X	X	X	X	X	X	X
A. verticillata								X	X	X	X	X
A. decurrens						X	X	X				
A. paradoxa							X	X	X			
A. saligna									X	X		
A. mearnsii											X	X

Prickly Moses

Golden Wattle

~January~

In southern Australia it is Mid-summer. Millions of Australians are enjoying their school holidays at the beach and extra low tides make rockpooling and snorkelling especially fascinating. On dunes and islands young seabirds hatch in burrows and sandscrapes. Hot, dry weather increases the risk of bushfires. In the south-west the end of the Nyungar Aboriginal season of Birak is marked by snakes and lizards shedding their old skins.

In the north, everything is wet. Torrential rains, heat and humidity characterise the Monsoon or Wet Season. Crocodiles move up flooded streams, and at Aurukun the season of Um Kapaak is marked by the movement of turtles into bays. Butterflies and swarms of other insects emerge. Big green frogs are found in toilets.

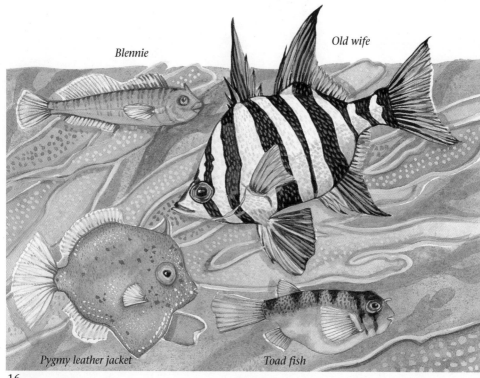

Blennie

Old wife

Pygmy leather jacket

Toad fish

January 1-8

Wetlands: magpie geese & Burdekin ducks build nests. **Coastal lowlands:** new shoots on native bamboo. **Woodlands:** flying foxes feed on lemon-scented gum flowers; first flowering of Darwin black wattle in NT; hawk moths feeding on lily flowers; pigeons & parrots feeding on ripening seeds of river oak. **Towns:** mud-dauber wasps storing spiders; dollar-birds in flock; rose-chafer beetles common. **Reefs:** barracuda come close to rocky islets. **Grasslands:** red-backed wrens in post-breeding flocks along coast; spear grasses heavy with seed. **Dry:** young Gould's goannas bask on bitumen roads; gall wasps lay eggs in river red gum leaves. **Mangroves:** first flowers on myrtle mangrove.

Dragonflies

Wetlands: tadpoles in ponds; dragonflies mating; ducklings walk to safety; rails move at night; nardoo is growing vigorously. **Woodlands:** echidnas seeking ant nests; ghost fungus on stumps; many feathers as small birds moult; bee-eaters feed young on dragonflies. **Beach:** toadfish & porcupine fish wash up; tiny transparent salps at high tide mark; blue swimmer crabs in surf; large sea-hares in rock pools. **Grasslands:** little ravens form large flocks. **Towns:** small skink lizards are hatching in gardens.

Your observations:

Magpie geese

Burdekin duck

17

January 9-16

Reefs: black-finned long toms are leaping. **Mangroves:** young black-tipped sharks cruise along mangrove edges; mangrove seedlings appear along river banks. **Beach:** mud crabs come up on high tide; lesser frigate-birds close to shore. **Wetlands:** snake-necked tortoises come up out of mud; mosquitoes common. **Rainforest:** white-tailed kingfishers feeding nestlings; round purple seeds of the white beech falling. **Woodlands:** yams are bright green; red-tailed black cockatoos feed on eucalypts; flying foxes & glider possums feed on bloodwood flowers. **Grasslands:** frillneck lizards feed on crickets. **Towns:** black cicadas singing in acacias. **Inland gorges:** native figs have unripened fruits.

Tern chick

Beach: bluebottles (Portuguese Man o'War) & velellas (By-the-wind Sailors) washing up; salmon in shallows; bronze whaler sharks patrol; tern & plover chicks are running. **Towns:** crimson bottlebrush flowering; Klug's & ringed xenica butterflies at peak in bushland remnants; fiddler beetles common in gardens. **Woodlands:** pardalote & yellow robin nestlings leave nests; painted acacia moths on indigofera; yellow rush-lilies flowering; grey mistletoe in fruit. **Wetlands:** male elodea flowers rise to surface in air bubbles; water striders are mating. **Ranges:** daphne heath in fruit.

Your observations:

Mud crab

January 17-24

Dry: termites swarming; wild orange has fruit. *Mangroves:* barramundi leave to swim across floodplains. *Beach:* large swarms of dragonflies. *Wetlands:* apollo jewel butterflies lay eggs on ant plants in melaleuca swamps; herring & archer fish work up freshwater streams. *Rainforests:* possums carry feeding young; red-eye tree frogs calling. *Woodlands:* phasmids on eucalypts; bright red fruits of creek cherry bob along streams. *Towns:* long-tailed finches nest-building; whiskered terns common on inland ponds. *Coastal lowlands:* long white flower spikes on ivory curl.

Woodlands: hyacinth & duck orchids flowering; seed pods on silver wattle open; magenta storksbill flowering; sweet bursaria at flowering peak; long-tailed wasps parasitising longicorn nymphs in SW. *Towns:* look up to see swifts & needle-tails feeding on flying ants as thunderstorms approach. *Beach:* paper nautilus shells & violet snails washing up. *Wetlands:* grebes build floating grass nests on lakes for second brood; daphnia water fleas develop large egg masses. *Ranges:* kestrels feed on emerging bogong moths.

Your observations:

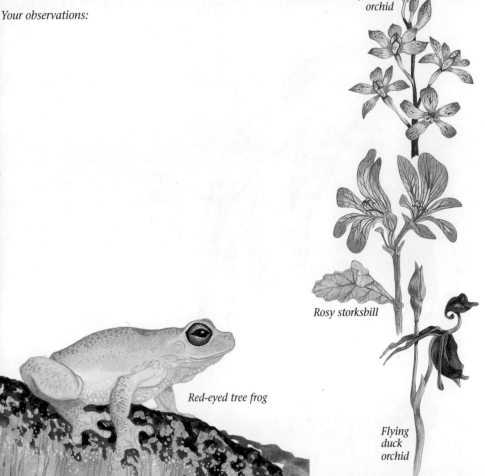

Hyacinth orchid

Rosy storksbill

Red-eyed tree frog

Flying duck orchid

19

January 25-31

Beach: night-herons & sharks wait for turtle hatchlings. **Dry:** ghost gums flower; bee-eaters common along creekbeds. **Towns:** figbirds & orioles feeding on damson plum fruits; brown crow & grass yellow butterflies emerge. **Coastal lowlands:** brush cuckoos move north; long pods on milky pine; two-lined dragons dig nest holes. **Woodlands:** marri seeds dropping; bush passionfruit flowers. **Wetlands:** brolgas on plains. **Mangroves:** high tides bring in many bait fish. **Inland gorges:** parakeelya flowering; white bush-apples ripen.

S **Wetlands:** whirligig beetle larvae pupate in muddy cocoons; swarms of midges above ponds. **Grasslands:** dandelions flower; jewel spiders making webs; stubble quail calling; kites prey on mice & locusts. **Towns:** wanderer butterflies & ladybirds common in gardens; look for grapevine caterpillars. **Woodlands:** snakes & lizards bask in warm bare areas; yellow rush-lily at peak flowering. **Beach:** look for brittle stars in rock pools; arrival of silver trumpeters along Tasmanian coast; shoals of mackerel are followed by barracouta, dolphins and gannets.

Kite

Your observations:

Grass yellow butterfly

Brown crow butterfly

Ghost gum

Jewel spider

Mouse

~February~

In northern Australia the Wet Season continues and Aboriginal seasons change depending upon local geographical differences. In Kakadu it is the middle of Gudjewg, the flood season, and egg time for the magpie geese. In Weipa, on Cape York, Prul Kun Njin, the first part of the Wet, has only just begun.

Around Alice Springs the hot, dry, desert weather is interrupted by occasional thunderstorms and lucky tourists see the spectacle of Uluru (Ayer's Rock) streaming with waterfalls.

Eastern coastal cities go through cycles of heatwaves, "cool changes", and electrical storms. Humid weather produces abundant insect life accompanied by predators such as swifts, spiders and wasps.

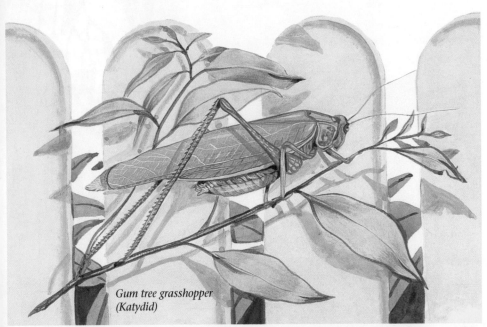

Gum tree grasshopper (Katydid)

February 1-7

 Monsoon forest: fungi in leaf litter. **Coastal lowlands:** pale-headed rosellas at nesting holes. **Wetlands:** water lilies flower in billabongs. **Mangroves:** estuarine crocodiles hatch. **Rainforest:** Gould's bronze-cuckoo calling in north. **Towns:** hairy cedar grubs invade houses; casemoth caterpillars on the move; grevilleas in flower; orb spiders build fluffy eggcases. **Woodlands:** green ant workers build new nests; red-winged parrots feeding on speargrass seeds; native cats [quolls] active at night; fungi in leaf-litter; white bush apple is ripe.

 Towns: red flowering gum with bright flowers; grey-headed fruit bats visit; dandelions flowering on vacant lots; many beetles around street lights. **Woodlands:** robber flies cruise along bush tracks; imperial white butterflies around; labyrinth spiders hatch; mistletoes flowering; tree frogs squeaking. **Grasslands:** horse mushrooms emerge along forest edge. **Beaches:** sand snail tracks in shallows. **Wetlands:** ribbon weed flowering.

Your observations:

Imperial white butterfly

Mistletoe

February 8-14

 Coastal lowlands: shining starlings flocking before migration. *Wetlands:* long-necked tortoises hatch from eggs; yellow fringe-flowers around temporary ponds; tadpoles & water boatmen are common. *Woodlands:* yam vines cover tree trunks; corellas feed on ironwood seedpods. *Dry:* large green frogs emerge after rain; dugite snakes lay eggs. *Towns:* red-collared lorikeets on paperbark blossoms; geckoes more numerous; fork-tailed swifts passing over. *Grasslands:* grasshopper nymphs emerge. *Rainforest:* young male tree-kangaroos disperse.

 Towns: grassdart butterflies on garden rock plants; fiddler & stag beetles common; young praying mantids on flowers; pimpernal flowers along footpaths; gum emperor caterpillars on gums & peppercorns; inky-cap fungi in grassy reserves; mole crickets are calling in back yards. *Woodlands:* fantails move down bush gullies; blackberries ripen along stream edges; blossoms on messmate stringybark. *Beach:* red & blue jellyfish in bay shallows.

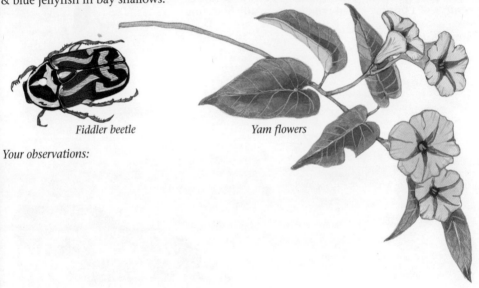

Fiddler beetle   *Yam flowers*

Your observations:

February 15-21

Wetlands: bulrush seeds disperse; some sandpipers leave Central Australia; wallabies move from swamps to higher ground; tailor-birds lay eggs; mosquito wrigglers in waterholes. **Coastal lowlands:** sweet smells from perfume tree flowers; koels & channel-billed cuckoos moving north. **Rainforest:** firewheel trees flower; Boyd's forest dragon lays eggs in damp soil. **Dry:** red scale insects on witchetty bush & mulga. **Woodlands:** flies appear; figs ripen. **Towns:** mangoes have new red leaves; look for rhinoceros beetles.

Towns: clothes moths emerging in houses; mud wasps building nests; ants on the move; tomatoes ripen in gardens; paspalum grass seeding; dingy swallowtail butterflies visit citrus trees; painted acacia moth caterpillars on apple & wattle trees. **Woodlands:** fire danger high; boletus fungi under pines; longicorn beetles emerge from wattle trunks; box mistletoe flowering. **Wetlands:** ferny azolla turning red in ponds; swamp lily flowering.

Your observations:

Mud wasp

Boyd's forest dragon

February 22-29

Mangroves: fruit bats arrive; stingrays common; mangrove snakes hunt on mudflats. **Wetlands:** reed warblers return to coastal haunts. **Dry:** Mitchell grass grows tall. **Coastal lowlands:** seeds of rose butternut trees on forest floor; many little eagles & swamp harriers about. **Rainforest:** strangler fig fruiting; vine reed cane has pink fruit. **Woodlands:** grass tree flowers attract feathertail gliders & bats; peaceful doves around puddles; musky rat-kangaroos start breeding in north Qld. **Inland gorges:** native ginger flowers; cycads have nuts.

Woodlands: gum emperor moths emerge; spitfire grubs of sawfly wasp attack new leaves on seedling gums; stick insects denuding treetop foliage; featherhorn beetles emerge; ivy-leaf violet at end of flowering period; long-leafed box & silverleaf stringybark flowering. **Towns:** aniseed weed & variegated thistle in flower on vacant land; cineraria moths in gardens. **Beach:** seaberry saltbush in berry. **Coastal scrub:** centipedes curled around eggs in teatree litter. **Wetlands:** *Galaxias* [small native trout] move down to estuaries to spawn; water boatmen migrate from drying ponds.

Your observations:

Fruit bat

Strangler fig

Gum emperor moth

~March~

In the north, the skies are clearing as rains abate. It is the Late Monsoon season. In north-east Arnhemland, winds are changing to the south-east, bringing the calm of Midawarr with its swarms of insects. In Darwin the waterfowl are laying eggs, while in Aurukun fruit bats have appeared in the mangroves (indicating the season of Kaap). Around Brisbane rainforest trees are fruiting.

Further south it becomes noticeably cooler towards the end of the month, and in Sydney some birds have already begun to fly north. In Melbourne and Adelaide pre-migration flocking has begun. Berries are ripening and marsupials are active.

Antechinus stuartii

March 1-8

Dry: ruby saltbush & wild tomato in fruit. *Monsoon forest:* crab's eye vine seeding. *Woodlands:* bar-shouldered doves in groups of 10 to 12 sit in dust bowls; black-throated finches nesting; partridge pigeons on roadside; green plum, billygoat plum & weeping paperbark in flower. *Towns:* yellow-throated miners feeding on grevillea; Darwin black wattles at peak of flowering; wasps building mud nests; casemoths appear; flocks of red-collared lorikeets. *Coastal lowlands:* large yellow fruits of native gardenia fall; black-faced monarch flycatchers move north. *Wetlands:* magpie geese lay eggs; red-capped plovers arrive; crinum lilies seeding.

Woodlands: young bandicoots out of the pouch; many birds now moulting feathers. *Coastal scrub:* kangaroo apple in berry. *Grasslands:* black field crickets on the move; tiny springtail insects floating in puddles after rain. *Towns:* leaf-curling spiders in gardens; case moth caterpillars moving; mason wasps store caterpillars in nests; soldier beetles on melaleucas. *Wetlands:* elodea waterweed stems break & migrate; many mayfly hatches; second brood of swamphens are running.

Your observations:

Leaf-curling spider

Kangaroo apple

Bar-shouldered dove

Case moth

27

March 9-16

Coastal lowlands: Torres Strait pigeons leave; leaden flycatchers & rufous fantails arrive from south; red-browed firetails nesting. **Wetlands:** double-banded plovers arrive from NZ; black bitterns nesting. **Woodlands:** broadleaf teatree flowers attract fruit bats; platypus seen in creeks when overcast; prostrate *Grevillea goodii* & golden parrot tree in flower; cluster fig in fruit. **Rainforest:** umbrella tree fruits attract fruit pigeons & starlings; small-eyed snakes around creeks. **Inland gorges:** red-tailed black cockatoos in coolibahs. **Dry:** ruby saltbush in berry; ironwood & bloodwood flowering. **Beach:** crisp tasty sea almonds on dunes.

Wetlands: many aquatic insects emerge as adults, attracting swallows & martins; river red gum flowers attract honeyeaters; daphnia waterfleas encyst in mud of drying waterholes. **Woodlands:** red wattlebirds flocking; cranberry heath & hop goodenia in full flower; symmomus skipper butterflies common. **Towns:** European wasps gather around swimming pools & soft drink cans [danger!]; gang-gang cockatoos feed on crab apples; canna lilies flowering. **Grassland:** thistle down blowing about. **Beach:** spinifex sends out new runners.

Your observations:

White-plumed honeyeater

River red gum

Umbrella tree

March 17-24

Wetlands: terns & migratory waders leave Central Australia; ibis, brolgas & Burdekin ducks on eggs. *Woodlands:* white-tailed rats feeding on candlenut nuts; sallee wattle has bright yellow flowers; red-winged parrots flocking; heliotrope in flower; ants rebuild nests. *Rainforest:* red-necked pademelon joeys emerge from pouch; white headed pigeons return; satin flycatchers move north. *Mangroves:* mangrove seedlings spear into mud; prawns on mud flats. *Dry:* skeletoniser caterpillars on gums; immature leaf-hoppers appear; buds on long-leafed corkwood. *Coastal lowlands:* helmeted friarbirds return; spangled drongos & dollar birds migrating north.

Woodlands: pied currawongs come down from mountains; brown-tailed moth caterpillars on mistletoe; cranberry heath still flowering; silver xenica butterflies around poa tussocks. *Towns:* emerald & anthelid moths on windows; bluebottle wasps dart around lawns; harlequin bugs on mirror bush. *Beach:* baby pipefish & cowfish in rock pools; octopus eggs wash up attached to sea-nymph grass; double-banded plovers arrive from NZ. *Grasslands:* speckled footman [heliotrope] moths on rushes.

Pipefish

Your observations:

Red-necked pademelon

Sea almond

29

March 25-31

 Coastal lowlands: common migrant butterflies lay eggs in cassia; bush hibiscus flowering; river turtles lay eggs. *Wetlands:* purple water lily spreading across pond surfaces; glossy ibis, yellow-billed spoonbills & pacific herons arrive; whistling ducks have ducklings. *Woodlands:* celery wood produces sprays of cream flowers; grasshoppers take wing; monitor lizards call from trees. *Inland gorges:* cycad fruit ripens. *Dry:* jewel spiders building webs in spear grass; ghost gums & ironwoods flower in centre. *Towns:* large flocks of black kites; white-tailed kingfishers moving north. *Rainforest:* Papuan frogmouths return to north Qld; large fruits of yellow walnut fall in tableland forest.

 Towns: tailed spiders in gardens; clara satin moth on windows; acorns falling; orb weaver spiders common; puffball fungi appear; starlings gain spotted plumage. *Woodlands:* antechinus marsupial mice active; first flame robin juveniles & females down from the hills; *Usnia* lichens show new growth; parsons band orchids flower. *Beach:* sea hares laying egg strings in rock pools; baby cunjevois wash up attached to sea-nymph grass; mangrove seeds are sprouting.

Mangrove seed

Your observations:

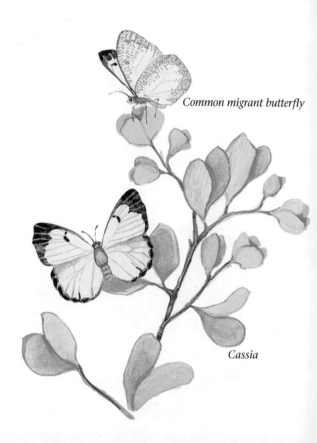

Common migrant butterfly

Cassia

~April~

In the south, Autumn is an extremely pleasant time of year.
Chilly mornings often give way to warm, but not hot, sunny
days. In Adelaide heavy rains at night bring out masses of huge,
silent swift moths, and fungi begin to appear in damp places.
Along the east coast wading birds begin their migration to Asia
and insect and seed-eating birds begin winter flocking. In
Sydney early flowering wattles are in bud.

In Brisbane macadamia nuts are falling, and further north the
end of the Wet is marked by strong winds. In the Kimberley
trade winds mark the beginning of the season of Goloruru. In
Kakadu the short season of Bang Gerang, or "Knock 'em down",
is marked by the flattening of tall grasses.

Curlew sandpipers

April 1-8

Coastal lowlands: Cooktown orchids flowering; orange migrant butterflies lay eggs on cassia leaves; pheasant coucals building nests; lovely fairy-wrens nesting; pallid cuckoos arrive; spotted harrier nesting. **Mangroves:** mangrove snakes withdraw from mud flats. **Monsoon forest:** sandpaper figs fruiting. **Woodlands:** last cuckoos leave; wild passionfruit in fruit; many purple line-blue butterflies. **Inland gorges:** Acacia dimidiata flowers on rock outcrops. **Wetlands:** platypus move overland during wet; little grebes have young; Asiatic waders are leaving. **Dry:** wing coral bean tree shedding orange-red seeds; yellow flowers on kapok bushes; slender grasshoppers in thousands. **Towns:** umbrella tree seeds ripen.

Grasslands: first field mushrooms; male flame robins join winter flocks on farmlands. **Wetlands:** masked lapwings flocking. **Woodlands:** grey fantails flocking; hawk moths common. **Towns:** leaves of deciduous trees changing colour; lemon bottlebrush flowering; oxalis common along footpaths; house centipedes active; inky cap fungi amongst long grass; in SW quendas [bandicoots] actively dig for insect pupae. **Beach:** flame robins feed on seaweed insects & crustaceans before heading north; sea snakes appear along southern coast; baby cowfish in rockpools.

Your observations:

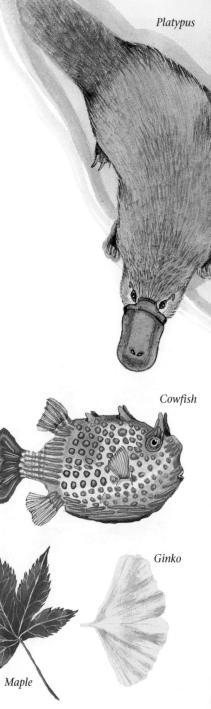

Platypus

Cowfish

Ginko

Maple

32

April 9-16

Mangroves: Sleeping dugongs float in channels. **Monsoon forest:** scrub fowl lay eggs in mounds. **Wetlands:** northern snake-necked tortoise lays eggs above waterline. **Woodlands:** billygoat plum in fruit; purple fig fruit on forest floor; rainbow birds lay eggs in soft earth tunnels; chestnut-breasted mannikin & pictorella finches in mixed flocks. **Dry:** processionary caterpillars build 'sleeping bags' in beefwoods; fuschia bushes flower after rain. **Towns:** cockroaches carrying egg cases; pink bloodwoods in flower. **Rainforest:** hedge-blue butterflies emerge. **Coastal lowlands:** cattle egrets arrive; black kites nesting; drongos move north; first flowers on red bloodwood.

Parsons
bands
orchid

Woodlands: manna gums flowering; parsons bands orchids flowering at peak; appleberry [bell climber] fruiting; dingoes mating; yellow-faced honeyeaters move north along wooded gullies; mealy amanita fungi in forest gullies; last blooming of *Wahlenbergia* [bluebell]. **Grasslands:** goldfinches in large flocks; slender parasol mushrooms among bracken. **Beach:** baby squids wash up. **Towns:** hawk moth caterpillars form brown pupal cases.

Your observations:

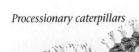

Processionary caterpillars

April 17-24

 Woodlands: agile wallabies & young move out of bush; large numbers of flying grasshoppers; young crows begging from parents; cocky apple ripens. **Coastal lowlands:** currawongs & fantails come down from tablelands; Alexander palms have bright fleshy seeds; tulip oak crowsfoot has cream blossoms. **Towns:** look up for flocks of swifts & needletails. **Dry:** hawk moths feed nightly on garden flowers; caper white butterflies on caper bushes. **Mangroves:** copper jewel butterflies common.

 Woodlands: wattle goat moths emerging; coral fungus on mossy ground; giant swift moths lay eggs at base of gums; black sheoaks flowering; woodswallows huddle on cold days. **Towns:** musk lorikeets active in street trees; shaggy cap fungi & fairy rings in parks & reserves; scarlet fly agarics under pines, birches & spruces. **Wetlands:** buds on swamp gums. **Beach:** many swamp harriers cross strait from Tasmania.

Your observations:

Fairy ring mushroom

Coral fungus

Shaggy cap

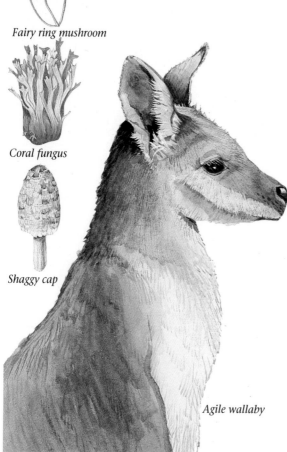
Agile wallaby

April 25-30

Inland gorges: spearwood begins flowering; magpie-larks flock in canyons. *Woodlands:* heteropogon & sorghum grasses seeding; spice bush produces poisonous red berries; young forest kingfishers group to dive on insects; salmon gums shed bark; goannas mating; southern rainbow bee-eaters arrive. *Rainforest:* black & white tit butterflies on orchid buds. *Mangroves:* box jellyfish migrate up creeks to spawn. *Dry:* tasty purple fruit of Burdekin plum ripen & fall; thorny devil lizards emerge on overcast days. *Wetlands:* morning glory has pink flowers. *Coastal lowlands:* fringed violet flowers; bunches of white flowers on tall candlenut.

Woodlands: sunshine wattle flowers in east; red ironbark flowers around goldfields; first rosettes of greenhood orchids; swift moths common; candlebark gums flower; ripe fruit on drooping mistletoe; small flocks of swift parrots pass over. *Towns:* purple-crowned lorikeets visit bush reserves; onion grass shows new growth; pin cushion hakeas flowering; soldier flies common. *Wetlands:* skinks & tortoises hibernate; black-fronted plovers flocking.

Your observations:

Box jellyfish

Swift moth

Black and white tit butterfly

~May~

Whales begin to migrate along the coasts to calve and mate.
In the south, Antarctic birds begin to appear, sandbars break as
swollen rivers break through to the sea, and in city parks
Autumn leaves swirl around parks and roadways. In Perth, cool
south-west winds predominate, and from Tasmania to
Queensland silvereyes move northward. In Adelaide vast masses
of seaweed wash up, along with the remains of other sealife.
Inland South Australia is much cooler.

In the north, the Dry Season has begun. In Kakadu it is the
season of Yegge, cool and humid, but further south at Katherine
the weather has already changed completely, and it is the
middle of the hot, dry, season of Jungalk.

Black-browed albatross

May 1-8

Woodlands: strong winds flatten grasses; white-browed woodswallows return; sugar-bag bees gather pollen from spear grass. **Wetlands:** magpie geese eggs hatch; black swans converge on ponds in centre; sarus cranes return. **Coastal lowlands:** yam vine leaves turn yellow; magpie-larks flocking. **Dry:** desert snails appear after rain; zebra finches nesting. **Rainforest:** king-parrots feed on sarsparilla fruit. **Monsoon forest:** banyans shed leaves. **Dry:** wild tomato & caustic bush flowering. **Towns:** straw-necked ibis return.

Wetlands: mature eels head out to sea to breed; many tadpoles in ponds. **Towns:** silvereyes come from Tasmania in large flocks; blackbirds feed on ripe cotoneaster, hawthorn & crab apple berries. **Woodlands:** last sightings of the imperial white butterfly; rain brings out many kinds of fungi. **Beach:** greenfinches feeding on sea rocket seeds; cuckoo-shrikes cross Bass Strait.

Your observations:

Hawthorn

Silvereye

May 9-16

Towns: dendrobium orchids & Darwin woollybutts in flower; dollar birds arrive. **Woodlands:** kites, crows & woodswallows follow fires; ants harvesting scale on young stringybarks; salmon gum sheds bark; bushman's clothes peg in flower. **Coastal lowlands:** red berries of yellow satin-ash attract many birds. **Rainforest:** large flocks of topknot pigeons feed on native nutmeg; pale yellow robins begin nesting; long white flower spikes on rusty oak in tablelands. **Wetlands:** dragon tree flowers along Kimberley creeks; brolgas return. **Inland gorges:** echidnas on move during evening. **Dry:** red mallee flowering; hawk moth caterpillars common. **Beach:** low tides, strong winds.

Beach: little prion seabirds washing up; sea cucumbers & nautilus shells washing in; swimming anemones in rock pools. **Woodland:** vegetable caterpillar fungi fruiting bodies emerge; caterpillars of hawk moth along stems of wattles; saw-sedge fruiting; shrike-tits moving through; peak of fungi season. **Grassland:** speckled footman moths common around rushes. **Towns:** oxycanus swift, chelepteryx gum and pink-edged twin emerald moths common on windows; tree lucerne flowering.

Your observations:

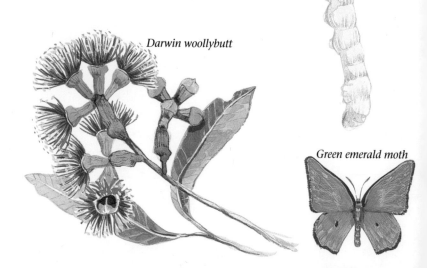

Vegetable caterpillar fungus

Darwin woollybutt

Green emerald moth

May 17-24

Mangroves: turtles courting; *Acacia holosericea* flowering. **Inland gorges:** dead finish, holly-leaf grevillea & indigofera flowering. **Coastal lowlands:** nectar laden flowers sprout from bumpy satin-ash trunks; pied butcherbirds nesting; forest red gum flowers attract fruit bats. **Rainforests:** cicada birds feed on grubs in cheese trees; fantailed cuckoos arrive; white blossoms clothe onionwood trees. **Towns:** bougainvillea flowering; small grasshoppers abundant; magpie-larks sit on overhead wires. **Woodlands:** black kites & whistling kites over burning grasses; many young galahs.

Woodlands: scarlet fly agarics, boletus & saffron milkcaps still common in pine forests; masses of yellow-faced honeyeaters moving north; magpie-larks flocking; luminous fungi on banksia logs; many orchid shoots are showing. **Wetlands:** tadpoles hatch. **Towns:** Mt. Morgan wattle flowering; leaf skeletoniser caterpillars on gum leaves. **Beach:** running postman in flower on back dunes; dolphins come into bays; pink robins cross Bass Strait; greenfinches feed on saltbush berries.

Your observations:

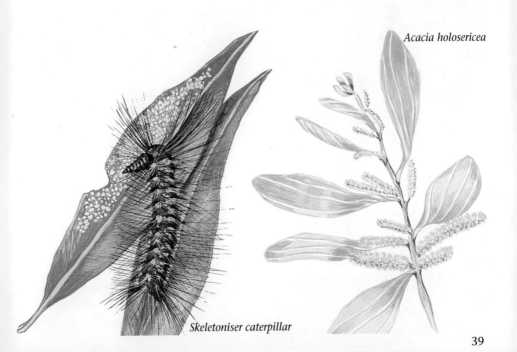

Scarlet fly agaric fungus

Acacia holosericea

Skeletoniser caterpillar

39

May 25-31

 Woodlands: red-flowering kurrajong sheds leaves. **Wetlands:** black swans are nesting. **Coastal lowlands:** brahminy kites & sulphur-crested cockatoos nesting; brown crow butterflies on mating flights. **Rainforest:** striped possums probe under bark of dead trees for grubs & beetles. **Dry:** large furry fruits on baobab trees. **Beach:** box jellyfish now scarce. **Towns:** beauty-leaf budding; white-breasted woodswallows & tree martins return; Cooktown orchids flower.

 Woodlands: mixed flocks of insectivorous birds pass down bush gullies; pink heath & flame grevillea flowering; ground thrushes active; Tasmanian blue gums & bushy yate flowering. **Towns:** last of the wanderer & admiral butterflies; yellow-tipped pardalotes arrive from Tasmania. **Wetlands:** cattle egrets in small flocks on flooded pasture. **Beach:** albatrosses enter bays.

Your observations:

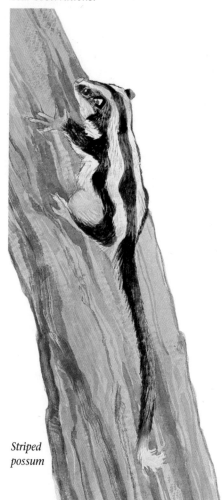

Striped
possum

Flame grevillea

Pink heath

Bushy yate

40

~June~

In the north, skies are filled with smoke as fires are lit. Black kites are everywhere, circling overhead and hunting along the front of burning grasses for animals forced from cover. The weather is cool and dry and many trees are flowering in the wide streets of country towns. It is the Bougainvillea Festival in Darwin; a cheerful mood pervades.

In the south, winter sets in — wet and wintry gales along the coasts wash up many seabird wrecks on deserted beaches. More fungi appear along with the first of the winter orchids, and many early wattles are flowering. Ponds are full of little water creatures. Evening fogs are filled with the smell of smoke from log fires. Morning frosts begin.

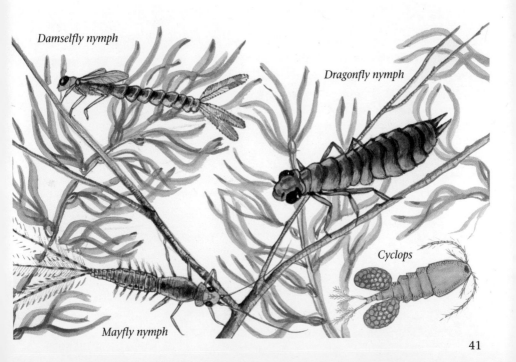

Damselfly nymph

Dragonfly nymph

Cyclops

Mayfly nymph

June 1-8

 Dry: longleaf corkwood, beefwood & dead finish flowering; sticky seeds on mistletoes. *Wetlands:* brolgas begin dancing; white star waterlilies on billabongs; river paperbark produces new silvery leaves. *Towns:* turkey bush in flower; oranges & mandarins ripen; weeping figs ripen; cheesewood seedpods release fluffy seeds; friarbirds come to flowering woollybutts; pardalotes & weebills in treetops; carpenter palms flowering. *Woodlands:* sand palm flowering; bush apples have shiny new leaves; king brown snakes common. *Coastal lowlands:* grove gum in flower.

 Woodlands: coral fungus on mossy ground; first nodding greenhoods & helmet orchids flower; first flowers on prickly moses wattle. *Grasslands:* rooting shank toadstool in long grass; yellow-rumped thornbills build domed nests in roadside trees. *Towns:* woolly bear caterpillars on grass. *Beach:* gannets diving off shore; black cormorants move in large flocks; cuttlefish eggs & dogfish eggcases wash up. *Ranges:* echidnas to be seen searching for mates.

Helmet orchids

Your observations:

Brolgas

June 9-16

 Coastal lowlands: brown tamarinds attract bees; white grevillea flowers; pheasant-coucals calling in dry swamps. *Dry:* mulga & witchetty bush flowering. *Wetlands:* long-necked turtles aestivate; darter young hatch. *Towns:* white cockatoo chicks hatch; mulberries have berries; kapok bushes flower. *Woodlands:* paperbark peeling off melaleucas; baby goannas about; doves come to water. *Inland gorges:* silver cassia flowering. *Monsoon forest:* estuarine crocodiles take dogs near rivers; leeches in hot mud puddles. *Rainforest:* bumpy satin-ash in flower. *Beach:* ospreys nest. *Mangroves:* flowers on red-flowering black mangrove.

 Woodlands: tall greenhood orchid & early nancy lily in flower; earth star fungi appear; cranberry heath in berry. *Towns:* first flowers on ornamental cootamundra wattle & red ironbark in South East; cottony cushion scale now common. *Grasslands:* herons, egrets, spoonbills & ibis flocking in flooded paddocks; lapwings laying eggs in ground nests. *Wetlands:* large flocks of pink-eared ducks on southern lakes. *Beach:* seals & dolphins come into inlets.

Cootamundra wattle

Your observations:

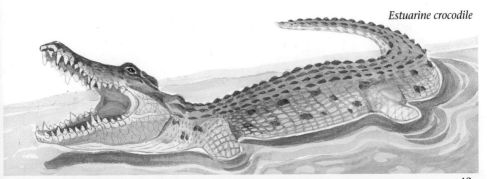

Estuarine crocodile

June 17-24

Dry: desert oak, spearwood & rusty saltbush flowering; many ants on wing; holly grevillea in seed. **Towns:** frangipani, jackfruit & weeping bottlebrush flowering; white cedars shedding bark. **Woodlands:** dingoes howling; yams ready for digging; nigidius & northern jezabel butterflies common; common ringtails have pouched young. **Inland gorges:** blue virachola butterflies lay eggs on orange fruit of strychnine bush; Mountford's wattle flowering. **Coastal lowlands:** striated pardalotes dig nesting holes; fruit bats squeak noisily; brown honeyeater & scaly-breasted lorikeets nesting. **Rainforest:** pied currawongs move in. **Wetlands:** barramundi plentiful.

Woodlands: boletus fungi in wet litter; billy-buttons & box mistletoe in flower. **Towns:** blackbirds feed on sticky seeds of pittosporum; many morning frosts; large flocks of silvereyes. **Beach:** after storms dogfish egg-cases, cuttlefish egg clusters and exhausted prion seabirds wash in; tiny porcupine fish trapped in rock pools; gannets & albatrosses close to shore. **Wetlands:** swans & coot now grazing on lake shores & neighbouring paddocks.

Your observations:

Northern jezabel
butterfly

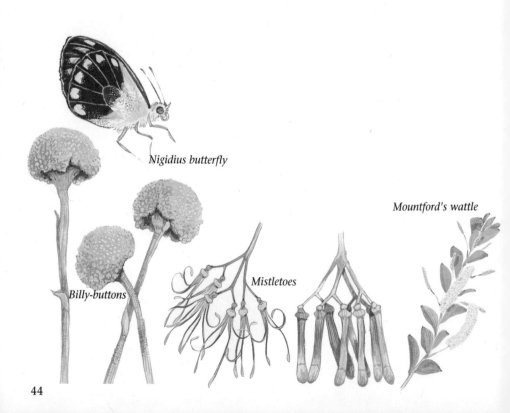

Nigidius butterfly

Mountford's wattle

Mistletoes

Billy-buttons

44

June 25-30

Woodlands: first broods of black & white aeroplane butterfly; Norton's oak in the wet uplands displaying small creamy flowers; double-bar finches nesting. **Inland gorges:** little bentwing & eastern horse-shoe bats hibernating; jewel beetles cluster. **Rainforest:** coppery brushtail possums feeding on *Acacia aulacocarpa*; fern wrens nesting. **Dry:** honeyeaters come to coral gums; saltpans dry out; umbrella bush & indigofera flowering. **Grasslands:** large flocks of chestnut-breasted mannikins. **Towns:** red-tailed black cockatoos feed on bloodwood seeds. **Coastal lowlands:** square-tailed kites at peak numbers; fibrous satin-ash has white flowers. **Beach:** sea-eagles nest.

Woodland: inky-caps, purple cortinars and flame fungi grow on mossy banks; long-leafed wattle in flower; shrike-tits tear bark off manna gums; yellow-tailed cockatoos on the move. **Towns:** painted acacia moth larvae eating geraniums; happy wanderer [hardenbergia] & jonquils flowering. **Grasslands:** many lambs are born; cows are fed grass hay; many foggy mornings. **Beach:** brown strapweed flowering.

Your observations:

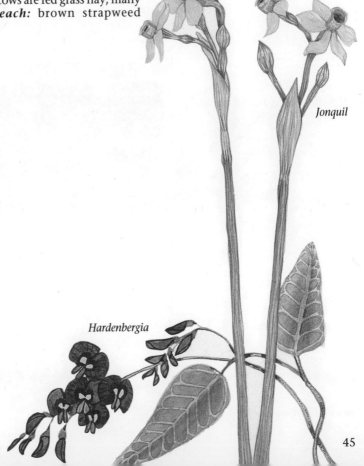

Ghost bat

Jonquil

Hardenbergia

45

~July~

It is the middle part of the Dry and the coolest part of the northern year. Mangroves are flowering along the coast and the first turtles are laying eggs. Many birds are already nesting.

In Alice Springs the temperature falls below zero at night.

In the south more wattles are blooming and several bird species are nesting, an indication that Pre-spring is beginning, according to our new calendar for Melbourne. Possums have tiny young in their pouches. Watch out for dive bombing magpies and lapwings.

Brushtail possum

July 1-8

Beach: green turtles lay eggs; wild pigs on beaches. *Coastal lowlands:* kapok bush, golden bouquet & forest red gum in full flower; grey shrike-thrushes nest in casuarina woodlands. *Reefs:* first humpback whales return to calve. *Rainforest:* large-billed scrubwrens nesting; native bees come to water; pygmy possums & blossom bats feed on bumpy satin-ash nectar. *Woodlands:* green plums flowering; poplar gums shed leaves; grey-crowned babblers nesting; new bark on ghost gums. *Towns:* brown crow & grass yellow butterflies lay eggs. *Inland gorges:* bauhinia flowers very sweet to taste. *Wetlands:* plumed whistling-ducks on tablelands. *Dry:* pardalotes in river red gums.

Pygmy possum

Woodlands: first calls of fantailed cuckoos; helmet orchids in flower; brushtailed possums have young in pouch; red box flowering in hills; leaves of bears ears daisy appear; juniper wattle flowering. *Grasslands:* jacky winter flycatchers return to nest sites; basket fungi on clay patches. *Beach:* albatrosses seen from headlands. *Wetlands:* frogs actively calling.

Your observations:

Bumpy satin-ash

July 9-16

Wetlands: blue & white water lilies bloom; apollo jewel butterflies emerge from melaleuca swamps. **Coastal lowlands:** Australian plane butterflies lay eggs on *Salacia chinensis* fruits; adult moth-butterflies emerge from green ant colonies. **Dry:** rattlepod flowers on dunes. **Rainforest:** red flowers of tree waratah on tableland treetops; kapok tree flowering. **Woodlands:** kurrajongs losing leaves; male agile wallabies boxing at dusk; turkey bush in full bloom along roads; rainbow lorikeets on flowering grevilleas. **Towns:** union jack butterflies feeding on mistletoe; flocks of sulphur-crested cockatoos.

Woodlands: golden wattle & prickly moses in flower; sugar gliders give birth; first flowering of chocolate lilies; yellow box seeding; flocks of sittellas pass through. **Towns:** cherry trees in blossom; casemoth caterpillars cutting sticks; earthworms crawl over paths after rain; snails active. **Wetlands:** rising waters cause ducks to seek new feeding & nesting areas; frog chorus on still nights; blooms of daphnia waterfleas in ponds & dams. **Beach:** Port Jackson shark eggcases wash up — some with live embryos; whistling kites patrol beaches; giant petrels close to shore. **Grasslands:** magpies collect nesting materials.

Your observations:

Prickly moses

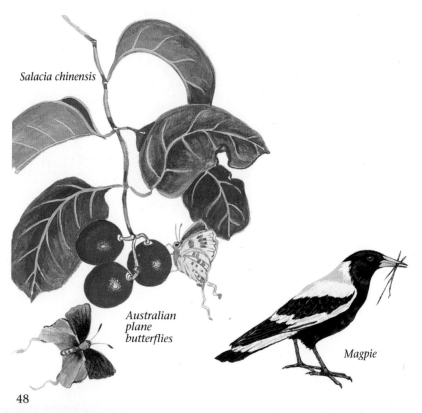

Salacia chinensis

Australian plane butterflies

Magpie

July 17-24

Woodlands: *Pandanus yirrkalaensis* fruit changes from green to red; bridled nail-tailed wallabies at peak of breeding; red-winged parrots feeding on wattle & kapok seeds; fruit bats very noisy. **Wetlands:** freshwater mangroves flowering; black swans have first cygnets; masked lapwings with running chicks; golden guinea tree flowers. **Coastal lowlands:** pheasant-coucals moult into breeding plumage; shining starlings return; scarlet honeyeaters & noisy friarbirds nesting. **Rainforest:** *Antechinus stuartii* mating; long pink flowers hang from *Hollandeae* in tablelands; almond tree leaves falling; first flowers on cadagi gum on forest edge. **Mangroves:** skinnyfish accompany barramundi. **Towns:** green tree snakes active; grasshoppers & moths abundant. **Beach:** oysters mature; brahminy kites feeding young.

Woodlands: satin bowerbirds on the move; maroonhood orchids flower; fire-damaged trees show epicormic growth; tree violet flowers. **Grasslands:** masked lapwings attack as chicks hatch; new cones on pine trees; little ravens flocking. **Beach:** squids washing up; silver gulls move to nesting islands; coast acacia flowers; more whistling eagles over coast; blue-green jellyfish close to shore.

Your observations:

Maroonhood orchid

Black swan

July 25-31

 Woodlands: milkwood flowers; bees feed on flowers of broad-leaved carbeen; speargrass now dead. **Beach:** flatback turtle lays eggs; sharks give birth; golden plovers, turnstones & common sandpipers return. **Rainforest:** wallabies feed on sweet potato; Lumholtz's tree-kangaroo joeys emerge from pouch; yellow-spotted honeyeaters & brown warblers nesting. **Wetlands:** lily heads have ripe starchy seeds; crocodiles sunning on banks. **Inland gorges:** bauhinias have bright red pods turning brown; long-tailed finches fledging; black-breasted buzzards nesting. **Coastal lowlands:** garlic vines flowering; white-throated honeyeaters, pratincoles & bush stone-curlews nesting; black cockatoos on the move. **Towns:** evergreen frangipani flowers.

 Woodlands: yellow-tailed black cockatoos seeking new feeding grounds; scrubwrens build nests; pink amanita fungus appears on moss; newly-flowering eucalypts attract many honeyeaters; noisy miners call loudly at dawn; silver, gold dust, blackwood, spreading and myrtle wattle flower; first nests of brown thornbill; tuans active. **Towns:** snowflake bulbs are flowering; eastern spinebills feed on new grevillea flowers; blackbirds begin territorial singing. **Wetlands:** lapwings on eggs. **Ranges:** scented sundews flower.

Your observations:

Eastern
spinebill

White-tipped reef shark

~August~

In the south, the weather is at its coldest, while along the northern coast it is already very hot. The weather is starting to warm in inland Australia. Native fruits are abundant in the northern woodlands and forests.

The first butterflies appear in the south and many ground orchids are in full flower. The cuckoos return and call continuously, as many more small birds begin nesting. Along the coast seal pups leave their colonies. Humans prepare vegetable gardens for Spring planting. Owls are nesting; listen for boobook owls in the bush.

Boobook owl

August 1-8

Woodlands: kingfishers excavating nesting holes in tree termite nests; red bush apple flowering; snakes laying eggs; apostle birds nesting; kapok bush in fruit; kurrajongs seeding. **Reefs:** turtles lay eggs. *Mangroves:* mangroves flowering. *Monsoon forest:* fernleaf grevillea, silverleaf paperbark & Leichardt tree flowering; little friarbirds feed on weeping paperbarks. *Towns:* palm dart yellow butterflies lay eggs on palm leaves; orange trumpet vine flowering. *Wetlands:* freshwater crocodiles begin nesting; pelicans & brolgas in large flocks. *Rainforest:* scrubfowls & brush turkeys attending mounds; yellow-breasted boatbills nesting; cicada birds & purple-crowned pigeons calling. *Coastal Lowlands:* figbirds nesting; brown-backed honeyeaters arrive.

Woodlands: early nesters now feeding young; new growth on eucalypts; cup fungi under large eucalypts; grasstree spikes in flower; hedge wattle & common hovea flower. *Towns:* daffodils flower; cupmoth cocoons on gum leaves; spotted doves building nests. *Grasslands:* spider hatchlings in long grass; young foxes playing; magpie-larks building mud nests — willie wagtails often build below them. *Wetlands:* weeping willows show first leaves.

Your observations:

Grasstree

Brush turkey

August 9-16

Coastal lowlands: first Torres Strait pigeons return to feed on figs. **Wetlands:** Latham's snipe return to marshes; herons, egrets & jabirus converge on waterholes. **Woodlands:** pandanus fruit fall to ground; dingoes giving birth; bottlebrush attract squirrel gliders; blue-faced honeyeaters feed on Leichardt tree nuts. **Towns:** citrus & stone fruit trees blossom; couch grass turning green. **Rainforest:** corky cricket-ball fruits fall from Kuranda satin-ash; grey whistlers call; possums & tree-kangaroos have pouched young. **Dry:** yellow-throated miners pairing. **Beach:** large influx of Asiatic waders. **Mangroves:** spiny mangrove flowers.

Woodlands: trim greenhood orchids, aotus & pultenaea bush-peas in flower; first painted lady butterflies in south; late black & silver wattles in full flower; king crickets [*Paragryllacris*] lay eggs in banksias; manna gums & long-leafed box in flower. **Beach:** shark eggs have visible embryos; sea-slugs [nudibranchs] lay egg rings.

Your observations:

Painted lady
butterfly

Pandanus tree
and fruit

August 17-24

Dry: large green pussytails; spiny-cheeked honeyeaters nesting; black kites more numerous; forkleaf corkwood flowering. *Beach:* very low tides expose crabs; double-banded plovers leave for NZ in full plumage. *Towns:* grape vines have new leaves; brown-backed honeyeater nesting. *Woodlands:* spangled drongos feeding on kapok blossoms; *Gardenia megasperma* flowers; black cockatoos on woollybutt in fruit. *Rainforest:* seeds of common lilly-pilly float downstream; topknot pigeons & black butcherbirds nest; Davidson's plum has ripe fruits like clusters of purple grapes; ginger in flower. *Coastal lowlands:* silky wattle flowering.

Wetlands: mosquito wrigglers abundant; early ducklings walk to water; reed warblers return from north. *Grasslands:* yellow pollen clouds come from pine trees. *Woodlands:* pallid cuckoos & shining bronze-cuckoos start calling; woolly bear caterpillars common; spider orchids flowering; spotted pardalotes build nesting tunnels for first brood; imperial white butterflies take wing. *Beach:* seal pups leave colonies; cormorants begin nesting; night return of Asiatic waders.

Mosquito wrigglers & pupa

Your observations:

Spotted pardalote

Lilly-pilly

August 25-31

Dry: rainbow bee-eaters return to centre; small grass-blue butterflies numerous. **Beach:** dugongs come close to shore. **Rainforest:** green ringtail possum young on mother's back; strangler fig has second fruiting — attracting koels & cuckoo-shrikes; little treecreepers call; Lesueur's tree frogs call along creeks; whipbirds in chorus. **Wetlands:** weeping teatree flowers attract friarbirds & fruit bats. **Woodlands:** grasstrees in full flower. **Towns:** eggfly & orchard butterfies common; orange blossoms; sunbirds nesting; figbirds feeding on palm fruits; drongos visit gardens; palm dart yellow butterfly caterpillars emerge.

Ranges: snows are thawing. **Woodlands:** sawfly grubs common on young eucalypts; yellow robins building; tree ferns unfold new fronds; purple coral-pea, donkey orchids & *Stackhousia* [candles] in flower. **Towns:** prunus plums in flower; cabbage white, meadow argus & small skipper butterflies appear. **Wetlands:** sandpipers & stints arrive on mud flats.

Your observations:

Cabbage white butterfly

Tree fern frond

Meadow argus butterfly

~September~

The bush comes to life! As the days become warmer more butterfly species emerge. The flowers of bush peas, lilies, and introduced weeds are visited by large numbers of insects. Mutton birds and Asiatic waders are arriving. The bush rings with the sounds of courting birds, frogs, and insects. Koala young leave the pouch. Pale office workers sun themselves at lunch time in cities.

Sturts's desert pea is flowering in a spectacular display in Central Australia.

Migrant birds are returning to northern Australia as well, where the weather is now hot and dry. In Aurukun it is the last part of Gnwor Mbwor, the time when emus lay eggs. In the Kimberley the rivers are now dry. In Katherine humidity is already building.

Koala

September 1-8

Woodlands: first koels & brush cuckoos calling; scarlet gum & northern kurrajong in flower; great bowerbirds repair & decorate bowers; Helena brown butterflies in jungle thickets. *Rainforest:* Victoria riflebirds & green-winged pigeons calling & displaying; spotted catbird, red-browed firetails & rufous shrike-thrush nesting. *Wetlands:* marsh sandpipers arrive in swamps; tortoises exposed as swamps dry. *Monsoon forest:* kapok tree produces red flowers; tree orchids flowering; jungle fowl have chicks. *Dry:* colony wattle & prickly wattle flower in centre. *Towns:* white cedars, African tulip & citrus trees are flowering. *Coastal lowlands:* Cairns birdwing butterflies emerge; butcherbirds, lemon-bellied flycatchers & olive-backed orioles nesting. *Mangroves:* large-billed warblers & Torres Strait pigeons nesting; flowers on small-fruited orange mangroves.

Woodlands: first flowering of ivy-leaf violet; leopard orchid, silver banksia & traveller's joy in flower; ringtail possums carrying young; skinks basking in sun; cherry ballart fruiting. *Beach:* yellow flowers of the boneseed weed throughout coastal scrubs; strong winds. *Towns:* admiral butterflies & red cockchafer beetles emerge; song thrushes build nests; cuckoos calling; new leaves on oaks.

Your observations:

Leopard
orchid

Admiral
butterfly

Travellers
joy clematis

September 9-16

Coastal lowlands: channel-billed cuckoos return to feed on figs; new shoots on grasses; Moreton Bay ash flowering. **Woodlands:** emus lay eggs; woolly aphids attack wild plum branches. **Rainforest:** noisy pittas start calling; mountain thornbills nest; grey whistlers have fledglings; grey-headed robins feeding young; land mullet lizards active. **Beach:** Siberian waders arrive; mullet reach great concentrations in bays. **Dry:** Gould's goannas sun-baking on roads; native orange flowering; black kites have left Central Australia. **Wetlands:** brolga courting dances begin; marsh terns breeding; barringtonias around billabongs lose leaves. **Towns:** lacewings lay eggs; bees begin swarming; spice finches breeding; orange blossoms in Central Australian gardens; ladybirds numerous.

Woodlands: hare orchids, pink fingers & purple hovea in flower; morel fungus on hillslopes; orioles calling; koalas mating; lomandra matrush has fresh spiky flowering heads; yam daisy flowering. **Towns:** emerald moths, especially red-lined geometers, on house windows; sweet pittosporum flowers attract bees; bird dropping spiders hatch. **Grasslands:** willie wagtails nest; magpie-larks feeding young; meadow argus butterflies abound. **Wetlands:** snipe return to long grass surrounding swamps.

Your observations:

Pink fingers orchid

Purple hovea

Willie wagtail

September 17-24

Woodlands: wallabies, kangaroos & bullocks moving around for green feed; Torres Strait pigeons feed on wild plums; brown snakes mating. **Dry:** many bloodwood 'apples'; parakeelya flowering beside roads. **Reefs:** reef fish courting; 'palola-type' polychaete worms swarm. **Mangroves:** prawn larvae migrate up mangrove creeks. **Beach:** *Trichodesmium* plankton rafts crash ashore. **Inland gorges:** manna on red gum leaves. **Towns:** African mahoganies in flower; koels call; pale-headed rosellas on grevilleas. **Coastal lowlands:** native cats [quolls] actively hunt with young; mass flowering of sarsparilla. **Rainforest:** black-faced monarch & little treecreeper nesting; new leaves on white cedar; sweet scent of native frangipani; bowerbirds & riflebirds displaying.

Woodlands: leaves of common bird orchid appear; mintbush, bauera, tetratheca & parrot peas in flower; cuckoo-shrikes feeding on caterpillars. **Mallee:** shield shrimps emerge as pools fill. **Towns:** tiger moths [*Arctiids*] common; bracelet honey-myrtle flowering in streets; green crab spiders on melaleucas. **Wetlands:** loud frog chorus. **Grasslands:** many grasses are flowering; capeweed in full flower. **Beach:** running postman flowering on back dunes & in coastal scrub. **Ranges:** immature King-parrots return to the mountains.

Your observations:

Onion weed

Kangaroo grass

Shell grass

King-parrot

September 25-30

Towns: silky oaks & kurrajongs flowering. *Woodlands:* cockatoos feed on woollybutts; flowering grasstrees attract feathertail gliders; fruit bats feed on green mangoes. *Rainforest:* main passage of satin flycatchers; Papuan frogmouths nesting; waterfall tadpoles in creeks; coppery brushtails eat bumpy satin-ash fruit. *Beach:* moon snail egg masses wash ashore. *Coastal lowlands:* taipans & death adders very active; eastern yellow robins nest; purple pom-poms on powder-puff lilly-pilly; warblers feed young brush-cuckoos. *Wetlands:* whimbrels return; freshwater mangrove flowers attract honeyeaters.

Towns: millipedes invade houses; apricots bloom; aphids on rosebuds; leaf-hoppers on gums; sallow wattles have large wasp galls; sawfly grubs now large; grey butcherbirds nesting. *Woodlands:* milkmaid lilies flower. *Wetlands:* pobblebonk & growling grassfrogs are on the move; swamphens have running young. *Beach:* sandsnails leave sand collars in shallows; muttonbirds [short-tailed shearwaters] return to nest.

Aphid

Millipede

Your observations:

Bullfrog

~October~

In the north, it is the early part of the Build-up to the Wet Season. Tropical colours seem to become more intense in the very humid air around Darwin and Arnhemland, and mosquitos breed. The waterholes have shrunk and many animals gather round them.

In Melbourne it is late Spring and flycatchers arrive from the north. In Brisbane scrub turkeys lay their eggs. In Adelaide the dawn chorus of birds is deafening, and in Sydney cicada song dominates the middle of the day. Lizards become active among the rocks. Bees are swarming and caterpillars create leaf damage on eucalypts. Many birds are moving south.

Blue-tongued lizard

October 1-8

 Woodlands: cocky-apple flowering; banded honeyeaters nesting; pythons laying eggs; dollarbirds arrive in Qld; white-breasted wood-swallows arrive. **Towns:** oakblue butterfly larvae feed on *Terminalia* shoots; tree-frogs call at night. **Monsoon forest:** *Vigna radiata* creeping pea starts to shoot among dry leaves. **Beach:** green turtles & loggerheads begin mating; big tides on northern coast. **Mangroves:** large-billed warblers nesting conspicuously. **Dry:** fairy martins nesting on cave walls; whitewood & billy-buttons flower. **Reefs:** giant clams breeding; marine stingers come inshore after northerlies. **Wetlands:** crinum lilies & bridal tree flower. **Rainforest:** pigeons, riflebirds & bowerbirds feed on fruit of bleeding heart; graceful & Macleay's honeyeaters nesting; white-headed pigeons & barred cuckoo-shrikes nesting.

 Woodlands: parrot-peas, fringe-lilies, sun orchids, love-creeper & late black wattle bloom; superb fairy-wrens nesting; morel fungi at peak. **Towns:** grass-blue, lesser wanderer & male common brown butterflies are plentiful in reserves & native gardens; lilacs in flower; starling eggs found on lawns; looper-worm [geometer] caterpillars in hedges. **Grassland:** green scarab beetles appear after rain; rufous songlarks come south. **Wetlands:** swamp paperbarks flower.

Your observations:

Lesser wanderer

Fringe-lilies

Love creeper

October 9-16

Woodlands: first tendrils of bush grape vine twine around cycad fronds; green plum & red bush apple in fruit; big numbers of red-tailed black cockatoos. **Wetlands:** magpie-geese flock to drying waterholes; white-winged black terns arrive; glossy ibis numbers peak. **Towns:** wasps drag huntsman spiders to nests; common crow butterflies lay eggs on oleanders. **Beach:** hermaphrodite barnacles start to form eggs after high tide. **Mangroves:** box jellyfish now free-swimming; flowers on long fruited spurred mangrove. **Dry:** seedpods on casuarinas; seeding wide-leafed wattles attract galahs. **Coastal lowlands:** singing bushlarks singing at night. **Reefs:** mass spawning of corals soon after full moon. **Rainforest:** white flowers on Queensland maple attract bees; bower shrike-thrush, spectacled monarch flycatcher & purple-crowned pigeon nesting.

Woodlands: tall sundews, grass trigger plants & riceflowers flowering; currawongs nesting; caper white & wood white butterflies emerge. **Towns:** yellow oxalis, wood sorrel & three-corner garlic on vacant land; sawfly wasp larvae go to ground; longicorn beetles emerge; pittosporum shield bugs lay eggs on pittosporum leaves. **Wetlands:** reed warblers return.

Your observations:

Wood sorrel

Tall sundew

Wood white butterfly

October 17-24

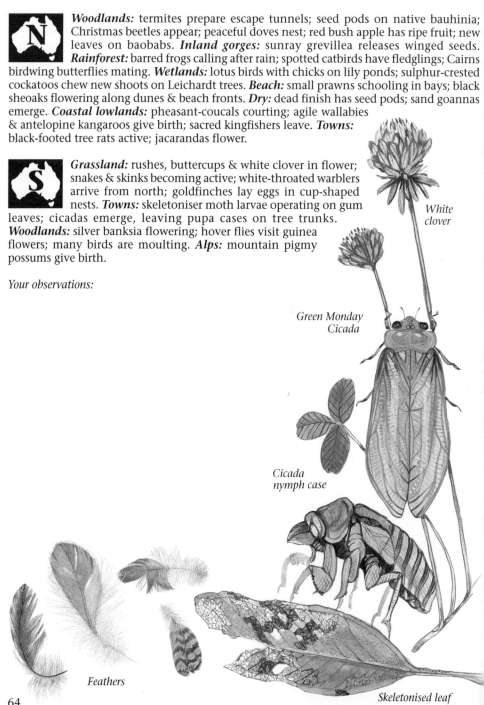

 Woodlands: termites prepare escape tunnels; seed pods on native bauhinia; Christmas beetles appear; peaceful doves nest; red bush apple has ripe fruit; new leaves on baobabs. **Inland gorges:** sunray grevillea releases winged seeds. **Rainforest:** barred frogs calling after rain; spotted catbirds have fledglings; Cairns birdwing butterflies mating. **Wetlands:** lotus birds with chicks on lily ponds; sulphur-crested cockatoos chew new shoots on Leichardt trees. **Beach:** small prawns schooling in bays; black sheoaks flowering along dunes & beach fronts. **Dry:** dead finish has seed pods; sand goannas emerge. **Coastal lowlands:** pheasant-coucals courting; agile wallabies & antelopine kangaroos give birth; sacred kingfishers leave. **Towns:** black-footed tree rats active; jacarandas flower.

Grassland: rushes, buttercups & white clover in flower; snakes & skinks becoming active; white-throated warblers arrive from north; goldfinches lay eggs in cup-shaped nests. **Towns:** skeletoniser moth larvae operating on gum leaves; cicadas emerge, leaving pupa cases on tree trunks. **Woodlands:** silver banksia flowering; hover flies visit guinea flowers; many birds are moulting. **Alps:** mountain pigmy possums give birth.

Your observations:

White clover

Green Monday Cicada

Cicada nymph case

Feathers

Skeletonised leaf

64

October 25-31

Woodlands: bush stone-curlews breeding; yellow stringybark, silky oak & swamp mahogany in flower. *Rainforests:* cassowary males tending chicks; coppery brushtail possums feed on wild tobacco; brown pines drop cherry fruits. *Wetlands:* lotus seeds ripen; brolgas dancing; magpie-geese prepare nests; azure kingfishers & blue-winged kookaburras visit waterholes. *Towns:* rainbow lorikeets feed on cadagi nectar; cuckoo-shrikes common. *Dry:* many cocoons on silver cassia; inland & black teatrees in flower; sawflies on red gums. *Mangroves:* Brugiera dagger-fruit fall into mud; small fish enter creeks to breed. *Coastal lowlands:* fruiting corkwoods attract figbirds; caper bush flowers. *Reefs:* Moreton Bay 'bugs' are breeding. *Beach:* ospreys with fledglings.

Beach: octopus & cuttlefish eggs wash up; young gulls leave nesting islands. *Woodlands:* rufous fantails & rainbow bee-eaters arrive from north; caper white butterflies begin south-westerly migration from ranges; cinnamon bells orchid flowering; leek orchids appear. *Grasslands:* kangaroo grass flowering. *Towns:* bees swarm; wasps searching for nest sites; old lady moths found inside.

Your observations:

Cinnamon bells

Old lady cloak moth

~November~

In the north the Build-up continues with extreme humidity, big tides, and some storms. Tension seems to mount as people anticipate the Wet Season. Barramundi move downstream for spawning. It is the middle of the season of Dhuludur in north-east Arnhemland and the scent of weeping paperbark is very strong. There are many winged ants about.

In Alice Springs the red gums shed their bark and begin to flower.

In southern Australia birds are kept busy feeding their young. Many birds are going through a post-nesting moult. Moths and beetles collect around lights. Holes appear everywhere as echidnas actively dig for ants.

Echidnas

November 1-8

 Rainforest: swift moths emerge near forest edge. *Coastal lowlands:* four-bar swallowtail butterflies emerge after first coastal storms; dollar-birds looking for nesting hollows; northern fantails building nests. *Reefs:* false trumpet shells & yellow balers exposed on bars; cay nesting of sooty & noddy terns at peak. *Wetlands:* freshwater crocodiles hatch; many ducks move into swamps; brolgas leave north Qld. *Woodlands:* green fruits on green plum; red bush apple ripe; young galahs hatch; male cones on northern cypress-pine. *Monsoon forest:* koels calling regularly. *Mangroves:* estuarine crocodiles begin nesting. *Towns:* milkwood, poinciana, pride of India & golden shower flowering.

 Woodlands: holes appear as bandicoots dig for grubs and echidnas search for ants; trillers move south; imperial white butterflies around mistletoe; phasmids in tree-tops; grasstrees & flying duck orchids in bloom; bramble in berry. *Grassland:* craneflies emerge around dams; black-shouldered kites attend harvesting; medic in flower; brown snakes emerge. *Towns:* plantain in flower along footpaths; irises flower; scarab beetles cluster around street lights; grassdart butterflies on yellow rockery flowers; lacewings emerge.

Cranefly

Your observations:

Plantain weed

Long-nosed bandicoot

November 9-16

 Wetlands: brolgas, jabirus, ibis, pelicans & magpie-geese ride the thermals; reed-warblers nest in bulrushes. *Coastal lowlands:* brown awl butterflies migrate to far north; cotton tree flowers; black butcherbird fledglings leave nest. *Reefs:* Moreton Bay bug larvae hitchhike on backs of jellyfish. *Inland gorges:* cicadas singing; flower caps of river red gum fall. *Towns:* seeds of beauty-leaf are ripe & falling. *Rainforest:* purple-crowned pigeons nesting; white-tailed rats eat fleshy blue nuts of Atherton oak; wompoo pigeons display; white flower spikes on Findlay's silky oak. *Woodland:* frillneck lizards mate; termites actively building; purple fruit on sandpaper fig; ironwood, ghost gum, carbeen & Darwin box in flower; billygoat plum & pandanus in flower.

 Beach: sea-hares lay eggs in rock pools. *Towns:* loquats ripen; spinebills visit weeping bottlebrush flowers in gardens. *Woodland:* fairies' apron flowers appear on swampy ground; nodding blue lilies bloom; wood-swallows nesting after migration south; Christmas mintbush flowering; first termites take wing; scarlet honeyeaters arrive from north. *Mallee:* mundarda [western pigmy possum] with young attached.

Your observations:

Leaf-hopper

Fairies' apron

Bottlebrush

November 17-24

Coastal lowlands: little red fruit bats feeding on mangroves; red beech & cottonwood flowering. **Reefs:** barracuda leave for deep water; terns diving for small trevally around reefs. **Mangroves:** barramundi & Sheridan's threadfin move back to mangroves for breeding. **Rainforest:** white-tailed kingfisher returns from New Guinea to nest in termite mounds; turpentine blossoms attract bats & gliders; grey albatross butterflies numerous. **Woodland:** large orange cicadas on casuarinas. **Monsoon forest:** Torres Strait pigeons feed on weeping fig. **Beach:** sargassum weed common.

Woodland: beard orchids on hillslopes; yellow box flowering; males of common brown butterfly appear; red ichneumon wasps common. **Beach:** shearwaters lay first eggs in burrow nests; red jellyfish appear in bays; gulls moult primary feathers. **Grassland:** scotch thistles flower; aphids & young leaf-hoppers on fruit trees. **Wetlands:** paperbark trees, [melaleucas], begin flowering.

Ichneumon wasp

Melaleuca

Your observations:

Barramundi

November 25-30

 Coastal lowlands: first Australian vagrant butterflies appear; scrub pythons active. *Reefs:* skinnyfish, spotted trevally, giant threadfin & turrum swim out to reefs. *Woodland:* frillneck lizards feeding on ground insects in new grass; rufous bettongs & bandicoots feed on emerging insects. *Rainforest:* cassowaries eat brown tamarind fruits; Helena brown butterflies lay eggs on saw sedge; red cedars have sprays of cream flowers. *Beach:* male catfish have mouthfuls of eggs; green & loggerhead turtles come ashore to lay eggs. *Wetlands:* pied herons & black bitterns return.

Towns: silky oaks, bottlebrushes & teatrees in flower in gardens; bee-flies & wasps are common. *Grassland:* capeweed & fireweed groundsel in flower; songlarks in full song; springtails ['lucerne fleas'] float in roadside pools; trillers moving south. *Woodland:* young butcherbirds hatch; good rains in catchments; Klug's xenica butterflies make first appearance.

Your observations:

Klug's xenica butterfly

Prickly teatree

Silky oak

~December~

In Melbourne, Adelaide and Perth it is early Summer, or Birak, as the Nyungar people of the South-west call it. This season is marked by banksias in full flower inhabited by squabbling honeyeaters. In Sydney the teatrees are full of feeding butterflies and jewel beetles. Bee eaters arrive in the south. Blooms of sealife occur in the shallows and many diving seabirds visit bays and estuaries.

In many places in the north the Wet Seasons have started. Cyclonic winds can develop and cause much damage on the coast, but inland and on Cape York the Build-up continues. New grasses appear where it has rained, and in Cairns Christmas lilies are flowering.

Rainbow bee-eater

December 1-8

 Woodlands: blue-tongue lizards give birth; tree frogs croaking after rain. **Wetlands:** water-lily seeds germinate; whistling-ducks on reservoirs; Burdekin ducks build nests. **Mangroves:** long thin seedlings develop on *Ceriops* mangroves; blind-your-eye mangrove flowers. **Beach:** box jellyfish wash out of creeks after rain. **Rainforest:** white flowers on creek cherries attract honeyeaters. **Inland gorges:** rainbow bee-eaters active along water courses. **Coastal lowlands:** oriental cuckoos arrive. **Reefs:** nesting of crested & lesser crested terns at peak.

 Woodland: teatrees, hop goodenia & guinea-flowers [*Hibbertia*] bloom; beard-heath [*Leucopogon*] in berry; orioles & white-throated warblers call; female common brown butterflies appear; white-lipped snakes emerge; bee-eater chicks hatch in nesting tunnels. **Towns:** late black wattle seeding in reserves; jewel beetles & scorpion-flies common on garden blossoms; wanderer butterflies visit swan plants in gardens. **Grassland:** narrow-leafed clover in flower.

Your observations:

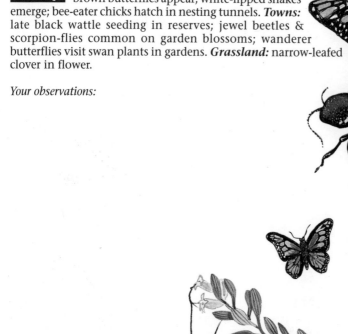

Wanderer
butterfly

Jewel beetle

Mountain
beard-heath

Scorpion fly

December 9-16

Woodland: new leaves on kurrajongs & planchonias. **Rainforest:** cockatoos feed on ripening banksias; golden tulip oak seeds litter forest floor; tooth-billed bowerbirds have fledglings. **Wetlands:** wandering whistling-ducks fight during courting; young tortoises in waterholes; jabirus lay eggs. **Coastal lowlands:** last sarus cranes head north; day-flying moths [*Alcidis*] become common; crimson finches feeding on hyptis thickets; more tree martins arrive from south. **Dry:** river red gums shed bark.

Beach: saltbushes flower; pipehorses, shark eggcases, sea-urchins, by-the-wind sailors [*Velella*] & blue-bottles [*Physalia*] are found on beaches. **Towns:** rove beetles, Christmas beetles & soldier beetles common on flowering melaleucas; jacaranda blooming; first needletails [swifts] pass over. **Woodland:** pygmy possums have young; saw banksia in flower; blue pincushions on hillslopes; lacewings hatch.

Your observations:

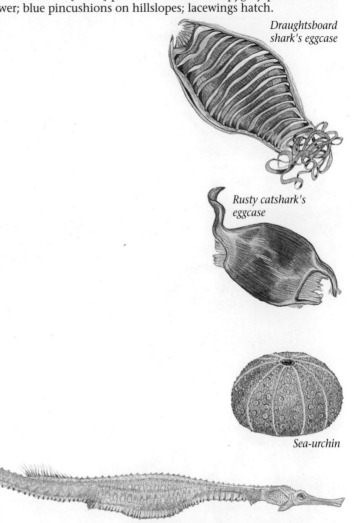

Draughtsboard shark's eggcase

Rusty catshark's eggcase

Sea-urchin

Pipehorse

73

December 17-24

Woodland: flying ants swarming. **Rainforest:** climbing pandanus in fruit; swarms of march flies; Queensland maple seeds fall; young riflebirds moult into adult plumage. *Wetlands:* crocodiles move upstream to breed on floodplain grasses; fantail-warblers [*Cisticolas*] & singing bushlarks build nests; white-necked [pacific] herons leave northern Queensland. *Beach:* large swarms of dragonflies; small prawns are schooling. *Dry:* coolibahs flower. *Mangroves:* mud crabs crush thick *Geloina* shells.

Woodland: tongue orchids, blue dampiera & Christmas mint-bush in flower; king crickets in old banksia logs; giant grey woodmoths emerge; pygmy possums have young. *Grassland:* kangaroo grass seeding; stubble quail call from long grass. *Wetlands:* water ribbons in creeks develop flowering spikes. *Towns: Diamma* blue-bottle wasps search for mole crickets. *Beach:* chains of salps in shallow waters on Tasmanian coast.

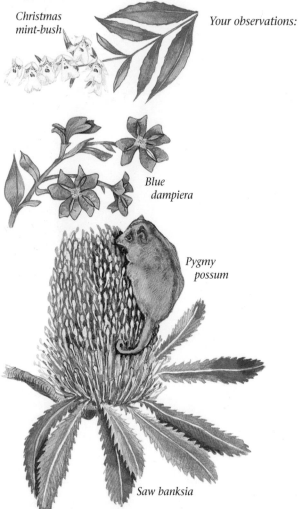

Christmas mint-bush

Your observations:

Blue dampiera

Pygmy possum

Saw banksia

December 25-31

Dingy swallow-tail butterfly

Monsoon forest: Terminalia seriocarpa has ripe purple plums. *Beach:* young tamarinds sprout along the beaches; turtle hatchlings charge to sea. *Coastal lowlands:* plumed whistling-ducks, grey teal & black ducks fly in to sit on the plains; koels move north; varied lorikeets flocking in flowering eucalypts. *Rainforest:* blue Ulysses butterflies feed on pink flowers along branches of butterfly tree; ivory bosswood flowers; huge swarms of march flies. *Woodland:* jewel beetles common on eucalypts. *Wetlands:* water rats feed on cane toads. *Mangroves:* thousands of mosquitoes. *Towns:* Christmas lily flowers; pink & yellow cassias bloom.

Beach: skuas & gannets feeding close to shore; skuas attack gulls, forcing them to drop food; white-fronted terns return from New Zealand; glassy shrimp hide with young in tunicate tests. *Woodland:* copperhead snakes & jacky lizards bask in sun; grass-tree & shaggy-peas flowering; kookaburras & sacred kingfishers feeding young. *Towns:* cidada chorus in oak-lined streets; dingy swallowtails around citrus trees. *Wetlands:* nursery web spiderlings by streams; water dragons sit on riverside rocks in south-east. *Alps:* mountain shaggy-peas flower.

Your observations:

*Jacky lizard
(tree dragon)*

75

WILDLIFE INDEX